Divine Self-Esteem

Divine Self-Esteem

Learning to Love Ourselves
the Way the Divine Loves Us

By Wade Galt

Possibility Infinity Publishing

Published and distributed by:

Possibility Infinity Publishing

Naples, FL

ISBN 978-1-934108-08-6

Dear GOD…

*Thank You for Creating Me
Exactly As I Am.*

*Thank You for Accepting Me
Exactly As I Am.*

*Thank You for Loving Me
Exactly As I Am.*

*Please Help Me Learn to Love and
Accept Myself the Same Way.*

Table of Contents

Who Are We to Criticize the Divine?

Imagine this… One day, the divine comes to visit you and takes on a human appearance. The divine says, "I just came by because I wanted to show you all the new creations I have made, and I'm interested in knowing what you think of them. I really like the creations a lot, but I always like to get a second opinion."

After looking at the new creations, you answer the divine like this… "Well, Lord. I know you are the creator of all that is. I also know you are the most powerful, loving, and all-knowing being in the entire universe, but I have to tell you that your artistic skills are really lacking. The neck on the giraffe is way too long. What happens if a giraffe gets an itch half way up its neck? The skunk just absolutely smells horrible. Couldn't you have come up with a more pleasant defense mechanism than that odor? And those bats are blind as hell. Pardon the expression, my Lord, but you asked for honest feedback."

This example, though it may never happen exactly this way, illustrates how limited we can be in perceiving things. I imagine if we told the divine these things that the divine would probably laugh because our answers would show such a lack of understanding on our part. We cannot completely appreciate the beauty and the uniqueness of the giraffe, the skunk, and the bat in the same way the divine does because we do not see the whole picture the way the divine sees it.

Although this example may not happen the way it is illustrated above, we do almost the exact same thing with the divine's creations. We may have even done so with the very same animals mentioned above. We say things like, "The world is just messed up;" "People are idiots;" "Life sucks;" "Those people are evil;" or "You are a jerk."

Sadly, for many of us, we are not able to see the perfection the divine sees, so we label things as bad, evil, and horrible. We assume we are right in our judgment of things and the divine is wrong to give and have unconditional love, life, and acceptance.

When we see and label things as wrong, evil, and bad, it's as if we are saying they are not divine creations. We attempt to isolate them and exclude them from the group of things we see as divine because we do not like something about them. It's as if we say, "The divine obviously created the things I like because I can understand and appreciate their beauty, function and purpose, so these things must be good. But the divine obviously did not create the things I can't understand or appreciate. Those types of things must be bad because I do not like them."

This doesn't sound so bad at first. We get to label things as "good" and "bad". We praise, appreciate, and honor the "good" things, while we belittle, take for granted, and dishonor the "bad" things. This all sounds fine while we are labeling other people, places, and things.

But one day we begin seeing the imperfections in ourselves, and things start to get uncomfortable. We notice we are out of shape or are not as attractive as we would like to be, so we call ourselves "fat" and "ugly." We notice we sometimes make mistakes or that we can be mean to other people, so we call ourselves "dumb" or "jerks." The list goes on, and pretty soon we find we have excluded ourselves from our divinely perfect "good" club.

We wonder if the divine still loves us because we can't seem to love ourselves. We now have a HUGE problem. We think to ourselves, "If the divine doesn't love and accept me as I am, how can anyone else?" (We assume that because we cannot love, understand, and accept ourselves that the divine and others cannot).

The thought that the divine would not love us becomes too great to bear. We must do something! This cannot be happening! So we begin to do all the same things we do when we think someone who is important to us doesn't like us. We try to manipulate them and change their minds. We beg, plead, curse, scream, bribe, rationalize, blame, and do anything else to get things back to "normal" (where they like us). Everything from "I'll be your best friend" to "You made me do it" becomes a fair tool to regain love, acceptance, and approval. The last thing we can stand is to be kicked out of our own tribe.

With the divine, we do the same things to try and manipulate the divine into liking us again. (Again, we assume the divine has stopped liking us). We create rituals to worship the divine (and we assume the divine wants and needs this). We make empty promises to the divine like, "If I get out of this, I promise…" (And we assume the divine believes this and can't see through our false promises). We blame things on others, "My parents were unloving to me, so I am this way" (and we assume the divine doesn't know the truth). Some might even say we make things up and create imaginary beings. "The devil made me do it!" (Only the divine knows for sure if there's a devil or not, but the divine most probably also knows the truth about our other excuses as well). *The amazing thing is that while we are doing all of these things to regain our lost love, acceptance, and approval, we don't even know for sure if we ever lost them in the first place.*

Our lack of ability to see the "divineness" in the things around us becomes its own punishment because eventually we begin to only see what's wrong with us rather than what is wonderful. If we could fully understand the entire divine design, we would probably be able to see how wonderful and divine we are. It appears, however, that while we are humans we may never be able to fully understand the divine design. This does not mean we cannot come to love ourselves.

We may not be able to understand the divine design or our purpose within it, but we can have faith that the divine created us out of love and loves us as we are. To this point in our evolution this seems to be our best tool. *With faith, we can learn to see ourselves with divinely loving, accepting, and understanding eyes.* It seems only a loving creator would have created a world where we can co-create almost anything we desire. And *if a mother can love her child and see past the "faults", can't the divine?*

None of us know and can prove for certain whether God loves and accepts us or whether God hates us and wishes to destroy us. So the question becomes, "How do we want to see ourselves and how do we want to experience our relationship with the divine?" Our answer to this question makes all the difference in the world.

How Do We Learn to Love Ourselves?

The remainder of the book is filled with questions for you to consider, pray about, meditate on, and explore. I invite you to include the divine in this process in whatever way(s) you know how. You might simply invite or ask the divine to guide you to the truth with a prayer or a request.

From here on out, this book is an experience based on your exploration and discovery as you seek the answers to the questions. I invite you to give the questions as much time and consideration as you need to come to a clear answer because the answers have huge implications. I also invite you to first make this an individual exercise with you and the divine. If you make this into a group discussion or debate, it may be much harder (or perhaps even impossible) for you to arrive at you own answers.

Once you feel good and confident about the answers you receive, you might find it easy to discuss your answers with others. I invite you to consider that your answers will probably be different than the answers of others you know, and that this can be a source of celebration and exploration rather than a competition over who is right.

My intention is that this helps you learn, understand, and accept whatever you need to in order to fully and unconditionally love yourself.

These Ideas Work For Me...

I wouldn't call them beliefs because I'm not attached to them. I'm not ready to kill or die to prove I'm right or that someone else is wrong. This is not dogma, so there's no need for anyone to argue. I'm not suggesting I'm right or others are wrong. I may be incorrect. I'm not saying I hold the only truth, the ultimate truth, or even truth.

This book is a collection of ideas that feel true to me, inspire me, and that work for me (based on what I can see in my life). I'd love to hear how these and other ideas work for you. I see this as a two-way learning relationship that we can both learn from. I'm not the teacher. You're not the student. We're just two people exploring ideas about the divine in hope of improving our lives and the world.

Please Accept My Humility and My Grandiosity

It is my only intention that this work brings you closer to peace, love, joy, happiness, and a greater connection with the divine. Please excuse my limitations as a writer as I attempt to do this. It is not my intention to make anyone feel wrong, uncomfortable, that they need to change, or feel anything other than fully loved, accepted and supported.

Please accept my grandiosity in wanting to address such a huge and important subject (and any apparent presumption that I'm right). Please also accept my humility in doing my best to make myself vulnerable by sharing something I think will make the world a better place. I honor all those people, organizations, religions, beliefs, rituals, and everything else that seeks to do the same.

At the same time, I remain excited, open-hearted and open-minded to seeing how we may grow, evolve, and change how we relate with the divine and each other to bring about even more peace, love, and happiness.

How Would You Love Your Children?

If you gave birth to children, and you knew you could always be the type of parent you wanted to be, how would you treat your children?

How do you think the divine treats the divine's children?

If you knew you could share all your love with your children and spend all the time you wanted with them without worrying about time or money, how often would you be with your children?

How often do you think the divine is with the divine's children?

What would you want your children to know about how you feel about them and how much you love them?

What do you think the divine wants you to know about how the divine feels about you and how much the divine loves you?

What would you want your children to learn about their self-worth and themselves?

What do you think the divine wants you to learn about your self-worth and yourself?

Would you want your children

to know they are very special?

Do you think the divine wants

you to know you are very

special?

Would you want your children to know they are loved and lovable?

Do you think the divine wants you to know you are loved and lovable?

Would you remember the names of all your children and bless them every day, no matter where they lived or how long it had been since they spoke with you?

Do you think the divine remembers the names of all the divine's children and blesses them every day, no matter where they live or how long it has been since they have spoken with the divine?

Would you tell your children they are wonderful and loved even though they sometimes do not listen to you?

Do you think the divine wants you to know you are wonderful and loved even though you don't always listen to the divine?

Would you encourage your children to take risks even though you knew this would mean they would sometimes fail?

Do you think the divine wants you to take risks even though this means you will sometimes fail?

Would you still love your children even when they make mistakes?

Do you think the divine still loves you even when you make mistakes?

Would you want your children to know that it's okay for them to make mistakes?

Do you think the divine wants you to know that it's okay for you to make mistakes?

Would you want your children
to know they are loved even
when they make mistakes?

Do you think the divine wants you to know you are loved even when you make mistakes?

*If you had the ability, would
you love your children
unconditionally?*

Do you think the divine has the ability to love you unconditionally?

If you would love your children unconditionally, can you think of any reason the divine would not love you unconditionally?

Would you love and accept

your children no matter what?

Do you think the divine loves and accepts you no matter what?

Would you be there for your children, no matter what?

Do you think the divine is

there for you no matter what?

If you think you can and do love your children with all your heart and soul, how much love do you think the divine has for the divine's children?

How Would You NOT Want to Treat Your Children?

Would you want your children to believe they are worthless?

Do you think the divine wants you to believe you are worthless?

Would you want your children to believe they are loved, but only if they meet certain requirements?

Do you think the divine wants you to believe you are loved, but only if you meet certain requirements?

Would you want your children to believe they are bad, but that if they apologized for being bad that you would accept or forgive them?

Do you think the divine wants you to believe you are bad, but that if you apologize for being bad that the divine will accept or forgive you?

Would you want your children to believe it's not okay for them to make mistakes?

Do you think the divine wants you to believe it's not okay for you to make mistakes?

Would you want your children to know they are not loved when they make mistakes?

Do you think the divine
wants you to know you
are not loved when you
make mistakes?

Would you love your

children conditionally?

Do you think the divine

loves you conditionally?

Would you accept your children only if they obeyed your rules and lived the way you said they should live?

Do you think the divine accepts you only if you obey the divine's rules and live the way the divine says you should live?

Would you condemn your children to eternal isolation and loneliness if they disobeyed you?

Do you really think the divine condemns the divine's children to eternal isolation and loneliness if they disobey the divine?

Would you be there for your children only if it served you or if it was not an inconvenience for you?

Do you think the divine is there for you only if it serves the divine or if it is not an inconvenience for the divine?

Would you be there for your children only if they praised you and told you how wonderful you are?

Do you think the divine is there for you only if you praise the divine and tell the divine how wonderful the divine is?

Would you be there for your children only if they gave you things?

Do you think the divine is there for you only if you give things to the divine?

Would you love your children, "only if"?

Do you think the divine

loves you "only if"?

Divine Self-Esteem

Divine Self-Esteem is based on a very simple idea – the idea that all divine creations are infinitely divine, good, wonderful, and loved.

If we break it down, it might look like this...

1) The divine created you.

2) All the divine's creations are divine.

3) You are divine.

4) Everything divine is good and wonderful in the eyes of the divine.

5) You are a good and wonderful in the eyes of the divine.

6) The divine is the source of all truth.

7) Whatever the divine sees as good and wonderful is, in fact, good and wonderful, regardless of what others might think.

8) You are a good and wonderful divine creation in the eyes of the divine, regardless of what others (including you) might think.

9) The divine esteems you and has a high opinion of you. (You are divinely esteemed).

10) You are worthy of Divine Self-Esteem. *

The only questions that remain are whether or not you can accept that you are worthy of Divine Self-Esteem and whether or not you can come to experience what it feels like to have Divine Self-Esteem (to share in the Divine's view of you as a wonderful divine creation).

Accepting Divine Self-Esteem

Many people have told us we are not worthy of any form of self-esteem, much less Divine Self-Esteem. We might have been told this by our friends, family, parents, strangers, the media, our religious institutions, and many other sources, including ourselves.

There are many ways to tell someone they are "worthless" or "unworthy" of love and acceptance, and we have heard them all. We have been told we're greedy, mean, ugly, fat, dumb, unloving, unkind, hateful, hated and many other similar things.

It is important to realize there is no better or more loving way to say these things, and that no matter how we sugar coat it, all of these labels suggest we are not worthy of divine love and acceptance. We can disguise and rationalize our lack of self-love with nice words (i.e. calling ourselves "unloving" instead of "judgmental"), we can use a group to validate our self-judgment ("according to the department of health, we are overweight, which equals fat, which equals ugly, which equals unlovable"), and we can even criticize the divine's wonderful creations (us) because we believe we are seeking to worship or please the divine.

No matter how we slice it, self-judgment is self-judgment. Many of our human religions have rules, social norms and codes of conduct that criticize, judge and put down the very same humans who create and continue to practice these religions. It seems strange that people would simultaneously believe God loves us and created the entire world for us, while still believing this same God does not love us as we are (and as we were created, by that same God).

We're basically saying and believing that we (one of the divine's miraculous creations) are flawed, bad, and wrong. Why do we believe such contradictory logic?

What's so scary about the idea that the divine loves us as we are? Are we assuming that if we can't accept parts of ourselves or certain behaviors that the divine will not either?

Is it scarier to think God doesn't accept us or that our peers and friends (who might belong to a certain organization) won't accept us if we don't agree with their beliefs?

Would we rather have the dogmatic (yet possibly still untrue) guarantee of a religion or organization that tells us we are bad and feel we know for sure that we are unworthy than take the risk and trust that the divine loves us exactly as we are?

Sometimes it feels safer to agree with the group than it is to stand alone. It can be more comforting to agree with a bunch of people who say we are unworthy and validate us for following their beliefs and rituals than it is to stand alone and connect directly with the divine to find out for sure. Even if the rituals and beliefs suggest the divine does not love us as we are or that we need to earn divine love, being in a group can sometimes feel safer, and we might choose safety over happiness.

In order to accept that the divine loves us unconditionally exactly as we are, many formal types of worship would have to be questioned, reformed or rejected. If we cannot get past our need for acceptance from the group, we probably cannot experience our acceptance of ourselves through the divine.

Eventually, it comes down to a very simple choice question. "Whose opinion of us do we value most, the divine's or the opinions of others?"

If the answer to this simple question is "the divine's", then we will not need groups to validate our self-worth. When we no longer need validation from others, we will find ourselves attracted to (or co-creating) groups of emotionally whole people (who have divine self-esteem and are growing in self-love daily) who get together to express their self-love, joy and gratitude to the divine and share their love, acceptance, and appreciation of each other.

Until we get past the need for validation from others, we will find ourselves attracted to (or co-creating) groups of emotionally incomplete people (with lower levels of self-esteem that are constantly decreasing) who get together and express their self-judgments, depression, and fear of the divine. We will compete for attention, approval, and acceptance as we attempt to be the perfect member of the group, in hope that someday, we will feel the divine loves us – even if we never come to love ourselves.

Jesus spoke directly to the divine and didn't seek the opinion of the tribe as a way to establish his opinion of himself. Buddha didn't asked the townspeople if they liked him. Lao Tzu never sought to win a popularity contest or create followers. Mother Teresa didn't ask others if they thought she was a good person for doing what she did.

When the approval of the group becomes more important than the opinion of the divine, religious and other organizations become little more than a bunch of people telling each other how sinful and terrible they are and how holy and wonderful they could be –" if only"...

When we come in as whole people, who know we are loved and valued by our divine creator, divinely inspired groups can become a powerful force that can transform the world.

Nobody outside of you can give you self-esteem - not your parents, not your friends, not your religion. But if you open up to seeing yourself the way the divine sees you, you may find that the answer to the question, "Am I a worthy and lovable person?" becomes as obvious as the answer to the question, "Am I a human being?"

Experiencing Divine Self-Esteem

In writing this book, I have been able to proceed "logically" from one step to the next because at each step I feel I do have the love, support, and acceptance of the divine. You may have experienced the same thing. It is also possible that you did not experience this. Maybe certain questions left you feeling uneasy or uncertain.

If I knew for absolute certain the exact steps or circumstances in life that were necessary for me to feel as divinely loved as I do, I would most certainly write them down and share with everyone. I regret to say I do not know them for sure.

At the same time, I do know what I have done to nourish and maintain the seed my mother planted when I was young and she somehow helped me understand that the divine loves me exactly as I am. Or maybe it's more accurate to say the divine planted the seed, and my mother was the first to help me bring it into my consciousness.

Either way, I have learned how I can stay in touch with the divine and stay open to receiving the guidance and nurturance I need. I use these tools when I need direction or answers or peace or anything else, and they work for me. (I have gone into detail about these tools in the book *GOD Can Be Your Coach*).

I offer this as a way to get in touch with the divine to get your own answers to the questions in this book, if you find it difficult to do so the first time you read. Ultimately, your answers, not mine, are what matter for you.

There are, of course, many other ways you can establish connection with the divine to receive guidance (i.e. prayer, meditation, silence, etc.). I simply offer this process as one way, in case you need it or can benefit from it.

Experiencing Divine Self-Esteem Exercise

➢ Set an intention to connect with the divine, and invite the divine to guide you in this process. *

➢ Close your eyes and silently breathe in and out.

➢ Do this for 30 seconds.

➢ Declare to the divine that you wish to feel the divine's love for you.

➢ **Ask the divine to help you see yourself through divine eyes.**

➢ **Ask the divine to help you love and accept yourself as you are.**

➢ Be still, listen and receive any guidance that comes to you.

➢ Breathe in and out for 30 more seconds.

➢ Thank the divine.

➢ Open your eyes.

* Repeat as often as necessary until you can fully feel the Divine's love for you (and whenever else you like).

* An intention is simply a desire you wish to have fulfilled. Setting an intention to connect with the divine simply means declaring a desire to have the divine connect with you for this exercise. This declaration can be made silently within you.

Answering Difficult Questions

- ➢ Set an intention to connect with the divine, and invite the divine to guide you in this process.
- ➢ Close your eyes and silently breathe in and out.
- ➢ Do this for 30 seconds.
- ➢ **Declare to the divine that you wish to know the truth, whether it will be comfortable for you or not.**
- ➢ **Ask the divine to help understand whatever you need to understand in order to apply the information you receive.**
- ➢ Be still, listen and receive any guidance that comes to you.
- ➢ Breathe in and out for 30 more seconds.
- ➢ Thank the divine.
- ➢ Open your eyes.

The Down Side of Divine Self-Esteem

As with everything else in life, there is what could be perceived as a down side that comes with having Divine Self-Esteem. It comes in the form of what some would call a responsibility and others would call an opportunity.

Once we begin to see ourselves through the eyes of the divine, and once we begin to experience and know how divinely wonderful we are, it becomes nearly impossible to not recognize that the same is true of everyone else. Everyone else is a wonderful divine creation and unconditionally loved by the divine.

Once we know this, we can no longer relate to people in the same way. In a moment we are fully aware of our sameness in being wonderful divine creations, we cannot treat another harshly, rudely, unjustly, or without appreciation. We cannot lie to them, blame them, dishonor them, or in any way control or manipulate them. If we truly see them as the divine sees them, we have no choice but to love and accept them exactly as they are, whether or not they are being the type of person we want them to be or doing the types of things we want them to do.

With unconditional love of another comes unconditional freedom for them. They can be whomever they want and we will love them, no matter what. (Many call this free will). *If we have very strong ideas about how we want life to be, how we want others to be, how we want others to treat us, or anything else, it will be very difficult (if not impossible) to love another or*

ourselves unconditionally. Our needs will get in the way of our love, and we will be forced to limit our love or put conditions on our love. We will love them or ourselves, "only if." This, of course, is not love, but manipulation.

If the divine loves us "only if", then the divine does not, in fact, love us, but simply wishes to control us. The divine has the ability to control us, and yet seems to allow us to make our own choices in life. If it's true that the divine has no unmet needs, it is possible for the divine to love us without condition. After all, there is nothing we have that the divine needs.

The divine doesn't need us to behave in a certain way, and the divine doesn't need to "trade" us divine love or acceptance in exchange for our obedience, money, worship, honor, praise, or anything else. The divine loves us unconditionally simply because the divine can.

Perhaps one of our closest human examples of this type of love is the love of grandparents. Many grandparents do not need their grandchildren to behave in certain ways. They just tend to love their grandchildren, spoil them with gifts and hugs and treats, and share time with them.

This kind of love can be tough for parents because social norms exist, and as parents, we often want to teach our children these norms and ways of relating. In the process, it can become very tempting for a parent to use their power or force to make a child obey. This may reflect the parents' need to have a well-behaved child or the parent may think they need to "do what's best for the child" or there may be many other needs. There is nothing wrong with this. It simply is.

The divine, on the other hand, has no such needs and can always love us unconditionally. We may not be able to do this for ourselves all the time, but the more we can love ourselves and others unconditionally, the more we can experience what it feels like to be divine.

What If I'm Wrong?

I know my mother and father love me, though I cannot prove it. I could list examples of ways they are loving towards me, but another could always argue, "How do you know for certain they are not doing these things for some other selfish reason?" Such questions do not interest me much because I cannot prove my answers, and I do not need to prove anything. I simply know. And yet, it is always possible I am wrong. I simply choose to live my live trusting I am correct.

I know the divine loves me, though I cannot prove it. I could list examples of ways the divine is loving towards me, but another could always argue, "How do you know for certain the divine is not doing these things for some other selfish reason?" Such questions do not interest me much because I cannot answer them, and I do not need to answer them. I simply know. It is always possible I am wrong. I simply choose to live my live trusting I am correct.

What If God Doesn't Exist?

The only thought that might concern us more than the possibility that the divine does not love us is the possibility the divine does not exist.

Personally, I believe with all my body, mind, heart, and soul that the divine does exist. My belief, however, could be wrong.

The only thing I can think of that might be more unfortunate than spending our lives trying to gain the approval of a god who already loves us would be spending our lives trying to gain the approval of a god who does not even exist. Considering this possibility, though it feels impossible to me, it becomes even more apparent how necessary it is for us to find esteem, love, and acceptance within ourselves.

If we, who know ourselves best, cannot love and accept ourselves as we are, who will or should? If, however, we choose to love ourselves throughout our lives, we will always know we have been loved...

Whether the divine exists or not...

Whether the divine loves us or not.

In God's Eyes

In God's eyes,
I am a unique and splendid creation.

In God's eyes,
I am remarkable and fascinating.

In God's eyes,
I am irresistibly lovable.

In God's eyes,
There's nothing I have to do to be acceptable.

In God's eyes,
I am perfect exactly as I am.

God's eyes always see truth.

Human eyes are not so reliable.

I think I'll trust God's eyes

Acknowledgments

Thank you God... for everyone and everything in my life. I am so blessed.

Thank you, Mom & Dad, for being such amazing parents and helping me experience such amazing love and acceptance. Some people say we see our creator through the lens of our experiences we have with those who raise us. Maybe that's why it's so easy for me to believe God loves me so much and why I have such a great appreciation for myself.

Thank you, Dr. Wayne Dyer, for being such a positive influence in my life and my work. I am blessed to have learned from you and been in your presence.

Thank you, Debbie Ford, for being such an amazing mentor, coach, friend, teacher and leader. Your impact on my self-esteem and self-love cannot be measured.

My intention is that all who read this book, including myself, will come to always experience what it feels like to know we are unconditionally lovable, unconditionally accepted, unconditionally worthy, and unconditionally loved.

About the Author

Wade has led retreats and personal growth workshops, authored books on spirituality, personal growth, finance, parenting, business growth & more.

He has worked successfully as a life coach, 4-day work week mentor, organizational consultant, computer trainer, sales consultant, executive coach, speaker, mental health counselor, management consultant, software designer and programmer, author, business analyst, financial counselor, and in many other capacities.

Wade has a Bachelor's degree in Marketing and a Master's degree in Mental Health Counseling Psychology.

He lives happily with his wife and children.

His email address is wade@wadegalt.com .

Author Blog & Website

You may visit Wade's blog & website at www.wadegalt.com .

Get the Audio for Free

If you like, you may get access to the audio version of this book for free.

To download it, go to GodEqualsLove.com/Audio.

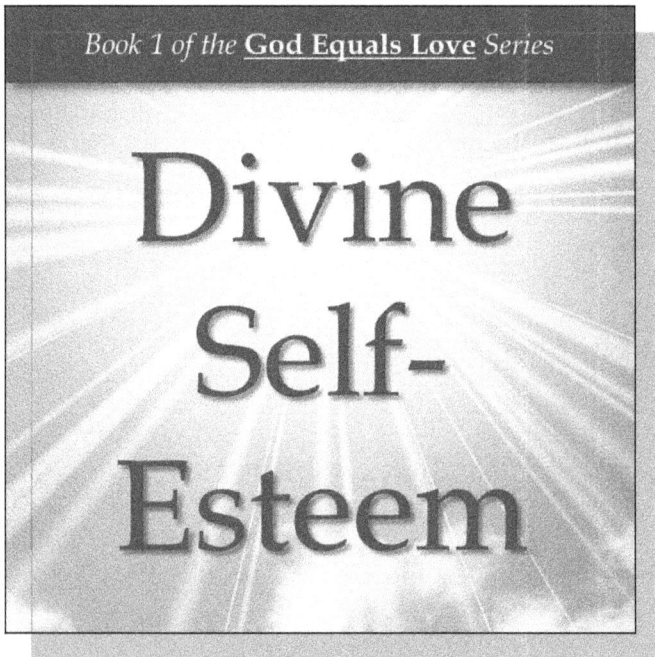

Book 1 of the **God Equals Love** Series

Divine
Self-
Esteem

Also by Wade Galt

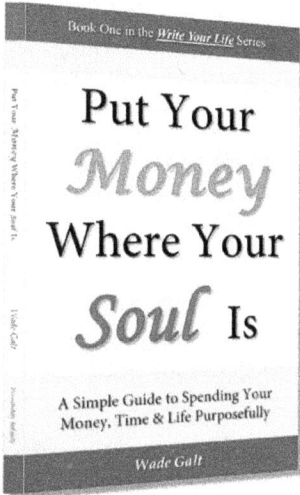

Put Your Money Where Your Soul Is

A Simple Guide to Spending Your
Money, Time and Life Purposefully

Learn how to free up additional time, money and energy by redefining your relationships with money, time, people, and things.

Simple strategies, exercises & tools help you make powerful changes with very little effort or struggle.

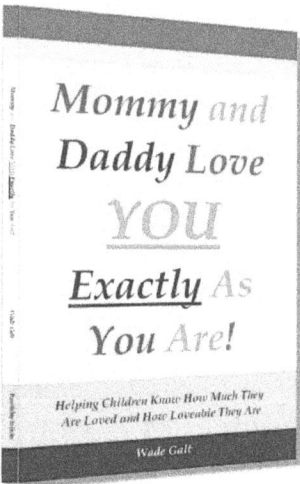

Mommy and Daddy Love You Exactly As You Are!

Helping Children Know How Much They
Are Loved and How Loveable They Are

My hope is that this book helps you...

1) Let your child or children know how special they are.

2) Remember how special your child or children are.

3) Understand how much your parents love(d) you, whether or not they ever shared this with you.

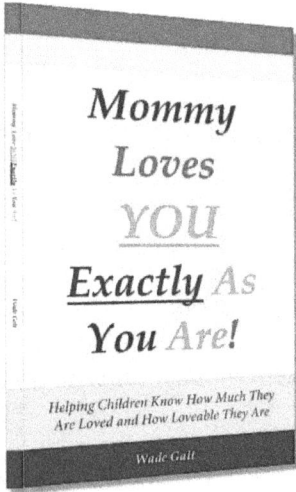

Mommy Loves You Exactly As You Are!

Helping Children Know How Much They Are Loved and How Loveable They Are

My hope is that this book helps you...

1) Let your child or children know how special they are.

2) Remember how special your child or children are.

3) Understand how much your parents love(d) you, whether or not they ever shared this with you.

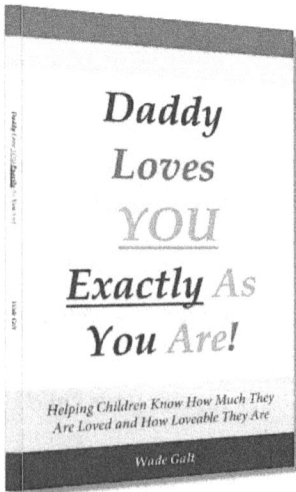

Daddy Loves You Exactly As You Are!

Helping Children Know How Much They Are Loved and How Loveable They Are

My hope is that this book helps you...

1) Let your child or children know how special they are.

2) Remember how special your child or children are.

3) Understand how much your parents love(d) you, whether or not they ever shared this with you.

The *God Equals Love* Book Series

(Free eBook Versions Available for All Books)

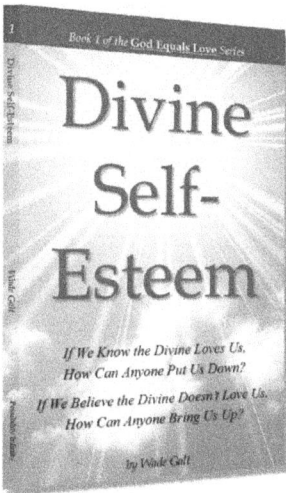

Book 1 - Divine Self-Esteem

Learning to Love Ourselves
the Way the Divine Loves Us

If we know the Divine loves us, how can anyone put us down?

If we believe the Divine doesn't love us, how can anyone bring us up?

Learn to see yourself through divinely loving eyes and catch a glimpse of the divinely-made miracle you are.

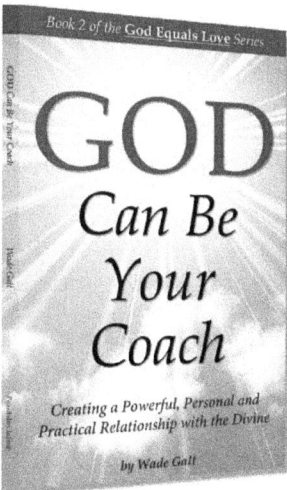

Book 2 - GOD Can Be Your Coach

Creating a Powerful, Personal and
Practical Relationship with the Divine

Create More Joy, Happiness, Love, Peace and Purpose in Your Life.

Learn One Simple Way to form a more powerful connection & relationship.

If You Knew You Could Connect with the Divine Anytime You Choose to Receive Guidance, Support, and Peace, Would You?

Will You?

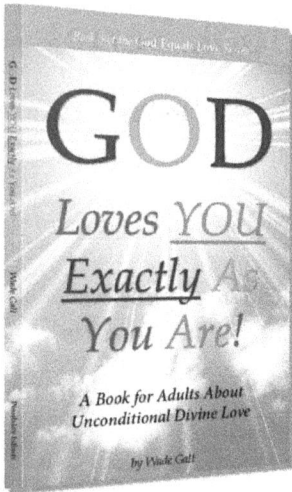

3 - GOD Loves You Exactly As You Are!

Understanding & Experiencing
Unconditional Divine Love

An Invitation to Consider & Experience the Life-Altering Understanding That You are Completely and Unconditionally Loved and Loveable EXACTLY AS YOU ARE!

What If God Loves You EXACTLY as You are?

How Would Understanding that Transform Your Life?

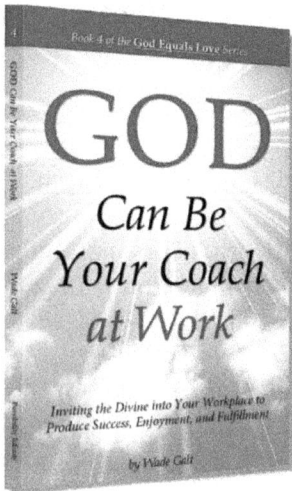

Book 4 - GOD Can Be Your Coach at Work

Inviting the Divine into Your Workplace to Produce Success, Enjoyment & Fulfillment

Few of us fully live our highest spiritual values in our workplace.

This is a source of frustration, shame, guilt & dissatisfaction for billions of us.

What if the divine actually wants us to experience life, love, joy, fulfillment, and abundance inside and outside our work?

What if the divine cares about our work simply because the divine cares for us?

This book is an invitation to work WITH the divine to create divinely inspired results for you and the world.

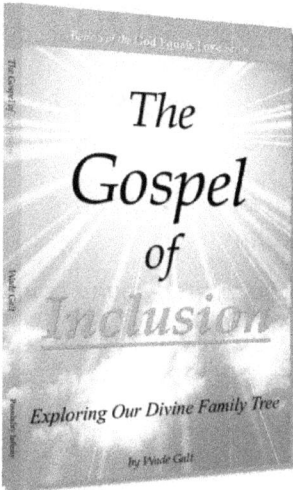

Book 5 - The Gospel of Inclusion

Exploring Our Divine Family Tree

Who is included in God's plan? Is it only people like me? Only people like you? What atrocities & apathy do we justify daily by declaring others are outside of God's chosen circle of people?

What if we really are part of one divine family? What would that mean? How would we have to change?

WARNING! Reading this book may lead you to (1) consider the possibility that we're all God's children and (2) do something about that. Proceed at your own risk!

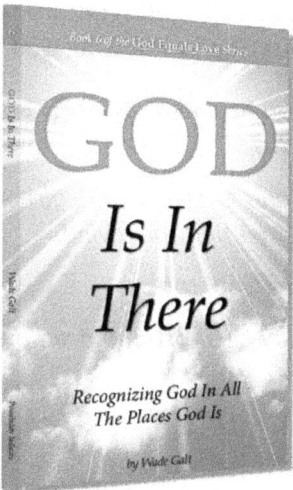

Book 6 - God Is In There

Recognizing God In All The Places God Is

If you could teach only one spiritual lesson, what would you teach?

What truth could you share that is so powerful, it would fundamentally transform the way others live?

There are a few core ideas that most spiritual traditions hold as true. Some believe that the most powerful and life-transforming truths are so self-evident and so obvious that all traditions agree about them.

This book contains one of those ideas.

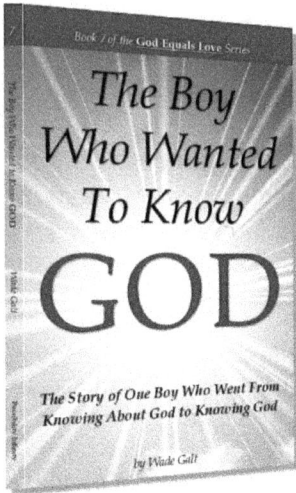

7 - The Boy Who Wanted to Know God

The Story of One Boy Who Went from Knowing About God to Knowing God

What would you be willing to do in order to meet God?

Join a curious and excited young boy on his journey to meeting the divine.

You might meet God, too.

The journey may be shorter and simpler than you think.

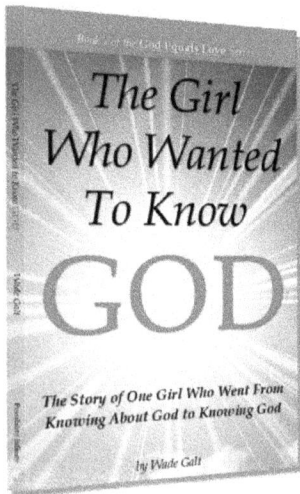

7 - The Girl Who Wanted to Know God

The Story of One Girl Who Went from Knowing About God to Knowing God

What would you be willing to do in order to meet God?

Join a curious and excited young girl on her journey to meeting the divine.

You might meet God, too.

The journey may be shorter and simpler than you think.

Translated into Spanish (More to Come)

Autoestima Divina

Aprendiendo a Amarnos De la
Forma en que Dios nos Ama

*Si sabemos que el Divino nos ama,
¿cómo podemos sentirnos mal con
nosotros mismos?*

*Si creemos que el Divino no nos ama,
¿cómo podemos sentirnos bien con
nosotros mismos?*

*Aprender a verse a sí mismo a través de
los ojos de amor de Dios y echar un
vistazo a el milagro hecho de Dios-que
eres.*

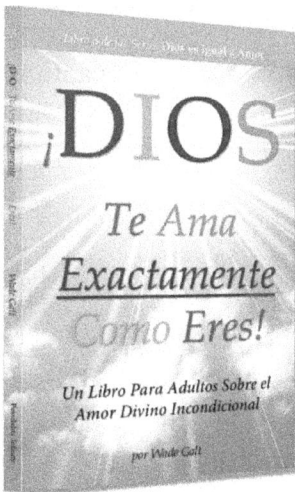

DIOS Te Ama Exactamente Como Eres

Un Libro Para Adultos Sobre el Amor
Divino Incondicional

*¿Y Si Dios te ama EXACTAMENTE como
eres? ¿De que manera ese entendimiento
transformaría tu vida?*

*Esto Es Una Simple Invitación... Para
Considerar y Experimentar... Un
Entendimiento de la Vida Alternativo...*

*Tú Eres Completa e Incondicionalmente...
Amado y Adorable... EXACTAMENTE
COMO ERES!*

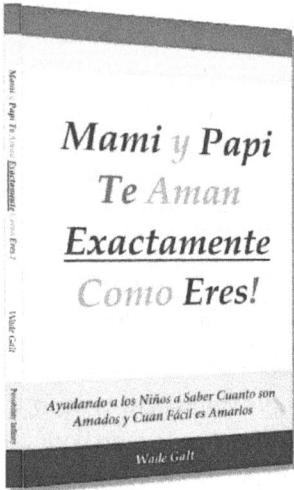

Mami y Papi Te Aman Exactamente Como Eres!

Ayudando a los Niños a Saber Cuanto son Amados y Cuan Fácil es Amarlos

Mi esperanza es que este libro te ayude a...

1) Hacer que tus niños sepan cuan especiales son.

2) Recordarte cuan especiales son tus niños.

3) Comprender cuanto te aman o te amaron tus padres ya sea que compartieran o no esto contigo.

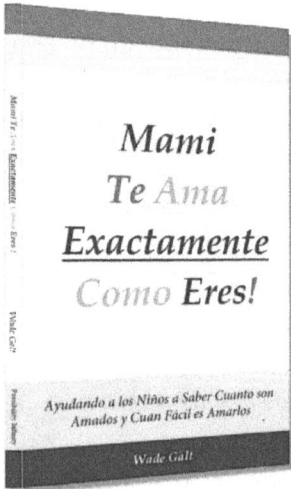

Mami Te Ama Exactamente Como Eres!

Ayudando a los Niños a Saber Cuanto son Amados y Cuan Fácil es Amarlos

Mi esperanza es que este libro te ayude a...

1) Hacer que tus niños sepan cuan especiales son.

2) Recordarte cuan especiales son tus niños.

3) Comprender cuanto te aman o te amaron tus padres ya sea que compartieran o no esto contigo.

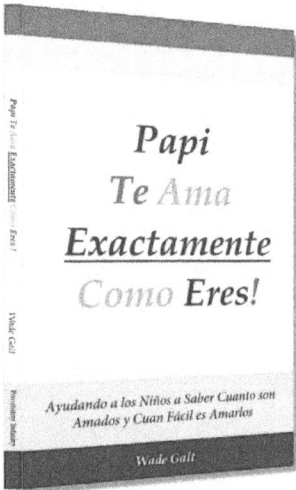

Papi Te Ama Exactamente Como Eres!

Ayudando a los Niños a Saber Cuanto son Amados y Cuan Fácil es Amarlos

Mi esperanza es que este libro te ayude a...

1) Hacer que tus niños sepan cuan especiales son.

2) Recordarte cuan especiales son tus niños.

3) Comprender cuanto te aman o te amaron tus padres ya sea que compartieran o no esto contigo.

To see these books and other books not listed here, visit www.wadegalt.com/books .

All profits from the sale of the GOD EQUALS LOVE books go to organizations and charities that seek to end unnecessary hunger and poverty.

New Book & Program Notifications

If you'd like to be emailed when we release new books, audios and other programs please visit www.wadegalt.com/notifiy to sign up for these notifications.

Share the Message & the Love

I hope this helps you see & feel how truly amazing and miraculous of a creation you are and how much the divine values you.

If you found the book to be helpful, would you please be so kind as to write a review on Amazon for the book or share the book on Facebook, Instagram, Twitter or other social media so others may benefit from it as well?

Even if it's a super-short review, every little bit helps.

Thank you so much.

If there's anything I can do to help you further with this work, please email me at is <u>wade@wadegalt.com</u> .

All my best,

Wade

www.ingramcontent.com/pod-product-compliance
Lightning Source LLC
Chambersburg PA
CBHW070643030426
42337CB00020B/4134